W9-BVO-034

Poems About FAMILY

BY America's Children

EDITED BY Jacqueline Sweeney

MARSHALL CAVENDISH
NEW YORK

For Frysians everywhere—especially Jetty, Hoyte, Froukje, Jantsje, Sjoke, Hiske, Germen, Jan, and Jaap—who have welcomed me with such kindness and integrity. J.S.

The publisher and editor would like to thank the following schools for opening their doors to us: Alden Place and Elm Drive Elementary Schools (Millbrook Central School District), Amenia and Millerton Elementary Schools (Webutuck School District), Barnum Woods Elementary School (East Meadow Union Free School District), Beekman, LaGrange, and Noxon Road Elementary Schools (Arlington Central School District), Boght Hills and Blue Creek Elementary Schools (North Colonie Central School District), Carrie E. Tompkins Elementary School (Croton-Harmon School District), Central Avenue Elementary School (Mamaroneck Union Free School District), Gardnertown Fundamental Magnet School (Newburgh Enlarged City School District), Germantown Central School (Germantown Central School District), Hackley School, Pawling Elementary and Middle Schools (Pawling Central School District), Scotchtown Avenue School (Goshen Central School District), Tesago Elementary School (Shenendehowa Central School District)

And with thanks to the art teachers (who worked so hard and were so wonderfully supportive): Christine MacPherson, Mary Molloy, Leslie Ann Pesetzky, Carole Pugliese, Mitchell Visoky, Nancy Woogen, Kerry Yankowich, Ilga Ziemins-Kurens

Special thanks to: Miriam Arroyo, Barbara Bortle, Ellen Brooks, Angela Butler, Pat Conques, Dotti Griffin, Anahid Hamparian, Peggy Hansen, Sandy Harvilchuck, Naomi Hill, Carol Ann Jason, Jennifer Lombardo, Mary Lynne Oresen, Joanne Padow, Carol Patterson, Theresa Prairie, Tracy Racicot, Ellen Ramey, Linda Roy, Nicole Sawotka, Jude Smith, Faye Spielberger, Bev Strong, John Szakmary, Glen White, Mary Ellen Whitely

Benchmark Books
Marshall Cavendish
99 White Plains Road
Tarrytown, NY 10591-9001
www.marshallcavendish.com

Series design by Anahid Hamparian

Library of Congress Cataloging-in-Publication Data
Poems about family by America's children / edited by Jacqueline Sweeney.

p. cm. -- (Kids express)
Summary: Poetry and art by children describing their feelings about family.
ISBN 0-7614-1507-6
1. Family--Juvenile poetry. 2. Children's poetry, American. 3. Children's writings, American. [1. Family--Poetry. 2. American poetry. 3. Children's writings. 4. Children's art.] I. Sweeney, Jacqueline. II. Series.
PS595.F34 P64 2002
811'.6080355--dc21

2002002262

Printed in Hong Kong
6 5 4 3 2 1

—Aimee Shevlin, *grade 3*

Contents

Teacher's Note

Imagine a classroom full of elementary school children bursting into applause upon hearing an announcement of an upcoming activity. Recess? Lunch? No. Writing poetry! Year after year, this is Jackie Sweeney's effect on students. I have been fortunate enough to witness this phenomenon over the last six years, as Jackie has conducted poetry residencies in the Arlington Central School District.

I study her as she teaches, trying to analyze her strategies. Although I have learned a lot from doing so, there is also some kind of magic at work here. Jackie is a modern-day alchemist, helping students turn their writing into something quite extraordinary.

What does she do? First, she convinces students that they are safe and their ideas are exciting. She focuses on free verse, providing structures through which she introduces students to poetic techniques such as sensory imagery, simile, metaphor, personification, and diction. At the same time, she invites students to surprise her with their own interpretations of these structures. She models extensively with examples from her own imagination and from the work of other students. Her samples are carefully chosen to counteract the notion that poetry treats only butterfly wings and flowers; topics range over every possible subject, from slithering pythons to pestering siblings.

Sensory perceptions are combined in surprising ways. Jackie might begin by asking students to picture a certain color and let it make them feel cold or hot or cool or warm. This is quickly developed into simile as she asks the students to consider how the color (let's say "red") is hot "like what?" As the students come up with their first tentative similes, Jackie immediately gets them to elaborate by asking questions until the child has produced: "Red makes me feel hot like a tomato on a white plate on a picnic table with the sun beating down on it on a summer day." Jackie exclaims, "Now I can see it!" and we are off on another year's excursion into poetry.

Peggy C. Hansen
Noxon Road Elementary School
Poughkeepsie, New York

Mom and Dad

My dad's eyes are like the green, green grass. My mom's lips are like a deer's tail. My dad's face is like a fire burning. My mom's hair is like ice cream with cherries on top. My mom and dad's best thing is a smile. (P.S. and that they got me a dog named snowball.) My mom's eyes are like the pools of dreams and my dad's nose is like a banana and I love them like an apple.

—Rachael Zofcin, *grade 3*

—Erin Bittner, *grade 2*

My Mom

My mom is like
a thunderstorm
that will never
stop. She feels like
thunderbolts coming
from the gods.
My mom can fly
with flying colors.
My mom has
power like
stone. She can
break a mansion
down in 10 seconds!
I love my mom!
When she feels sad
she makes it
rain. My mom is
the greatest.

—Anthony Mullen, *grade 3*

I feel lonely when I think of my
mom's heart. It's as empty as a glass
without water. It's just like
a car on a highway then the wheel
pops. I loved my mom really much.
When she was little
she was so pretty. She had long black
hair with brown eyes and beautiful
dresses.

—Kelvin, *grade 2*

—Lauren Thomann, *grade 2*

Happy's Good

When I'm happy
I feel like a princess
that just got declared
queen. I feel like I
just got cuddled up in my
mom's arms with my
head rubbing against her
soft shirt on a cold winter
day when the wind is
blowing hard.

—Sara, *grade 3*

—Laken Flynn, *grade 3*

Mad at My Brother

When I'm mad I don't speak
to him. I feel sad. Sounds like
him crying. Looks like a flood.
I wish he would forgive me.

—Rachel Sidney, *grade 2*

Baby Brother

My baby brother is like a monster.
He tries to eat me up.
He chases me in the living room.
He loves to play dominoes.
He likes Elmo. He likes to spit.
He is wild. He likes to eat Oreos.
Sometimes when he is sleeping
he looks like a ripe peach.

—Robert Facchin, *grade 3*

Fury of Fangs, Rage of Fire

When my big brother
insults me, I feel like I want
to grow fangs and bite him.

—Travis Norman, *grade 4*

—Anna Gagnon, *grade 4*

The Saddest Thing

The saddest thing was when my daddy
went to get pizza and he didn't come back
for an hour. It felt like I would never
see him again.

When my dad came home I ran up to him
and said I love you and I hugged him.
I was so happy and that pizza tasted
very good.

—Colleen Spang, *grade 2*

—Anna Gagnon, *grade 4*

The Saddest Day

The saddest thing that
happened to me was
when my dog died.
My mom was crying
so hard she was wet
as an ocean full
of fish.

—Zachary Stillman, *grade 3*

Sad Ant

When I'm sad
I feel like an ant
that was in the water
trapped under three jars.
And the water has
black smoke. And the water
is freezing cold. Maybe
someday I will bite into a
juicy apple. Perhaps my family
will come and get me.

—Zachary Coto, *grade 2*

Grandpa's Gift

My grandpa gave this to me. It
is so special like a diamond.
When I look inside my special cup
I feel like I am in outer space.
My cup makes me
think of my Grandpa.
I wish he was alive.

—Humberto Karner, *grade 2*

Happiest Sister

My sister feels happy when she goes with my dad but I don't. I feel like a sandwich.

—Esteffany Lopez, *grade 3*

—Kara Fallon, *grade 3*

—Taylor Connor, *grade 5*

A Day with Your Dad

The most
spectacular thing
is going to
the movies with your
dad
no matter what you see
like
Armageddon
Titanic
or MIB
it's like a dream
come true
it's like Christmas
a day
that you can't
wait for it
to come to life
I wish
everybody
could have this
day
with their dad.

—Evan Odynsky, *grade 3*

Auntie Gordon

Auntie Gordon is like a crab
scurrying along the beach.
He is like a plaid shirt
that my dad wears to work.
He is like a rainstorm
on a foggy day,
like a peanut that I ate
last night with dinner.
He takes me to a place I
only go with him. I don't
know where it is though
it is like a cloudy beach.
Auntie Gordon is kind of
my uncle but not exactly.

—Kate Wesley, *grade 3*

—Christoph Rufer, *grade 5*

My Crazy Dad

My crazy dad blasts the music.
He sounds like a wild animal.
He snores like Hannah. He beeps
at my friends to be cool.
He wrestles with my brother.
He gets mad at the cat if
the cat's on the table.
He sits in his chair watching
cable. He eats red meat.
He's a policeman and if somebody
gets wise he locks up the bad guys.
He tells you to do something
'cause he's lazy and if you don't
he'll get crazy.
But he's my dad.
I have to love him.

—Tara Martin, *grade 5*

—John Donnelly, *grade 3*

The Loudest Peep

My bird peeps all day
to get attention.
When he sings La Cucaracha
he sounds like a siren.
It makes me feel cold inside.
He peeps when
my cat wants him for breakfast
because he is nervous.
I wish I had ear plugs.

—Calyn Wiese, *grade 4*

Sadness

Bucky please don't die.
I love you so much.
You are 18 and I will
be very sad when you
die. You are the best
cat a kid can ever have.
When you die I will be
an apple without carmel.

—Chris Patchey, *grade 5*

—Joseph Battaglia, *grade 3*

—Martin Rodrigues, *grade 5*

—Lindsey Bennett, *grade 2*

—Alison Simmons, *grade 2*

—Rachel Moynihan, *grade 2*

—Savannah Rose, *grade 2*

Sammy My Dog

When my dog Sammy died
it felt like a part of me had
died. I loved that dog.
He smelled like my dad's
carpet. The color of his
fur was gray like my
grandma's hair. Sometimes
I feel like I am in one
dark room.

—Amelia Repko, *grade 3*

The loneliest thing
is me. My dad
works like a gladiator
and he's never home.
When my mom puts
me in my room I feel
like I am in a dog cage.
I am lonely when I go
outside. I feel like I am
on a small island with no one.
I am definitely the loneliest
thing in the world.

—Robert Breitenbach, *grade 4*

—Gaby, *grade 2*

The Smelliest Feet in the World

The smelliest thing is my dad's feet after being
in his boots all day long. They smell so bad
that they will kill you. His feet smell like
rotten cheese. Even when he takes his shower
his feet still smell. His feet smell like a
rotted animal. He is the smelliest
bird in the world. Sometimes he puts his
feet in my face. I almost die.

—Dominick Manco, *grade 2*

Karl the Snapper

Three years ago I didn't
know how to snap.
I felt like mud and
old cheese.
Then my poppy showed me
how to snap.
Now I snap all day
at school.

—Karl Wendover, *grade 2*

My dad's caring is like a river that keeps
going
all night.

—Adam Boese, *grade 4*

—Chelsea Mailler, *grade 5*

The Kitchen Cabinet

My hiding place is under the sink.
I hear the pots and pans jingling.
It smells like perfume. I feel
comfortable and sometimes if
my dad never finds me I
fall asleep in a big pot.
I like to play drums
if nobody is in the kitchen.
This place makes me
feel safe by myself.
When my mom does the
dishes I pretend I am
singing to the rain.

—Tayla Fauntleroy, *grade 3*

Spider in Pudding

I love sleeping.
Sleeping is like a slug.
It moves like a spider
in pudding.
It's like I'm hanging
from a rope with
nothing to do. I wish
I could sleep all day.

—Nikki, *grade 3*

When I'm angry a tiger
comes out like when my brother
hits me. Then I chase him like in
a huge zoo. My teeth are as sharp
as a knife and I catch him and . . .

let him go because I just
couldn't eat my brother.

—Eddie Kelly, *grade 5*

—Makaylla Bowdren, *grade 5*

Madness Motions

Madness makes me feel like a lion
charging at someone. Madness is red like
a pot of soup burning over the stove.
Madness sounds like a storm near the
ocean. Madness looks like a giant wave
hitting a small ship. Madness feels
like a big bumpy rock that can't be
broken. Madness is a group of people

breaking up.

—Tycho Sicker, *grade 2*

—Harley Tucker, *grade 3*

The Moment

Last year my grandma died.
I never felt so bad
in my entire life.
I felt like my whole
life was about to end.
My dad felt so bad he
told me that he wanted
to just stop—and that's
exactly how I felt except
it showed in my heart—
it was pounding and
breaking into these little
pieces. The next day
we went to her funeral.
Everyone was wearing black.
My heart was pounding harder
and harder but then suddenly
it stopped and something told me
she was in the right place.
Then instead of black
I saw a rainbow.

—Nicholas Marr, *grade 5*

—Maria Barbini, *grade 3*

White Iceberg

I am a white
iceberg.

I have to tell you something.
I will not be here forever.
One
Hot
Sunny day
I might melt and
never come back.
So next winter
try to make me again!

—Fred Alger, *grade 2*

—Holly Mulhern, *grade 2*

Yellow Sun

I feel good enough to help my sister reach
the sun. She is so little that she
had me put her on my shoulders.
I could feel her squirming and kicking.
She reached so high
I felt like blowing up a yellow balloon
and letting go
so she would grab it and say,
"I have the sun." And then I
remembered how it feels to reach
the sky.

—Jessica Leslie, *grade 2*

—Lauren Marino, *grade 2*

Art credits

Anna Gagnon cover, 8, 9
Jessica Koralus title page
Aimee Shevlin copyright page
Erin Bittner 5
Lauren Thomann 6, back cover
Laken Flynn 7, back cover
Kara Fallon 10
Taylor Connor 11
Christoph Rufer 13
John Donnelly 15, back cover
Joseph Battaglia 17
Martin Rodrigues 17
Lindsey Bennett 18 (left)
Alison Simmons 18 (right)
Savannah Rose 19 (left)
Rachel Moynihan 19 (right)
Gaby 20
Chelsea Mailler 22
Makaylla Bowdren 25
Harley Tucker 26
Maria Barbini 27
Holly Mulhern 28
Lauren Marino 29

Author index

Kangaroos

The most myterious thing in the world
Is how a kangaroo gets its pouch for its baby.
Its like you are in bed
With the covers tucked up to your neck.
It makes you warm in the middle of the winter.
It feels like I am in a hole full of animal fur.
I am so comfy.
I fall asleep in a flash.
It is the most comfyest thing in the world.
I wish I could switch with a baby kangaroo.
I wish I would never fall out.

By Brandon
Soechtig

—Brandon Soechtig, *grade 4*